Radical Robots

Can You Be Replaced?

George Harrar

Simon and Schuster Books for Young Readers
Published by Simon & Schuster Inc., New York

In association with WGBH Boston,
producers of NOVA for public television

SIMON AND SCHUSTER
BOOKS FOR YOUNG READERS
Simon & Schuster Building
Rockefeller Center
1230 Avenue of the Americas
New York, New York 10020

SIMON AND SCHUSTER
BOOKS FOR YOUNG READERS
is a trademark of
Simon & Schuster Inc.

Manufactured in the United States
of America.

10 9 8 7 6 5 4 3 2 1
10 9 8 7 6 5 4 3 2 1 (pbk.)

Library of Congress
Catalog-in-Publication Data
Harrar, George.
Radical Robots: can you be
replaced?/George Harrar.
(A NOVABOOK)
"In association with WGBH Boston,
producers of NOVA for public television."
Includes index.
Summary: Examines the design, construc-
tion, and applications of robots, discuss-
ing what they can and cannot do and the
extent to which they can develop their
own intelligence.
1. Robots – Juvenile literature.
[1. Robots. 2. Robotics.]
I. WGBH (Television Station:
Boston, Mass.).
II. NOVA. (Television program).
III. Title. IV. Series.
TJ211.2.H37 1990
629.8 '92 – dc20
90-31572 CIP AC

ISBN 0-671-69420-0
ISBN 0-671-69421-9 (pbk.)

I dedicate this book to my mother
and father.

Special thanks goes to the publish-
ing and design staff at WGBH, in
particular my editor, Karen
Johnson, as well as designer,
Douglass Scott; photo researcher,
Elise Katz; and artist Mark Fisher.
Thanks, too, to Nancy Linde, for
generous assistance, and to the
staff at Simon and Schuster's
children's book division.

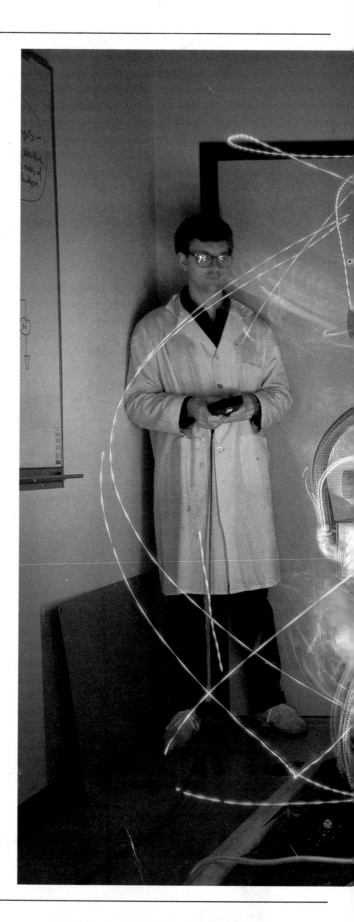

Title Page:
**The diner of the future might
be manned by a robot.**

Contents Page:
**A student tests a robot at the
Stanford University computer
lab.**

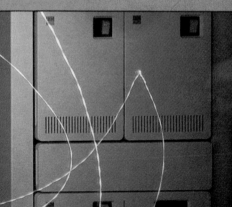

Contents

Why Robots Can't Tie Shoelaces But Can Go to Mars

Smear Vaseline on the lenses of an old pair of glasses. Put a boxing glove on one hand and strap the other behind your back. Now try to tie your shoelaces. That's how it feels to be a robot in the year 1990.

Robots are like toddlers – right now they can't do all the things that older children or adults can. But they are growing up fast, and their potential is amazing!

Independent robots will go to Mars before humans do. Robots will run our homes – cleaning, guarding, mowing, teaching, entertaining. Robots will travel to faraway places as our substitutes, sending back images of all they see and descriptions of all they touch to make us feel as if we are there. Robots will play with us, remember for us, in many cases think for us. Robots are already building more robots like themselves – in effect, reproducing.

What will make the robots of the 21st century truly awesome will be advancements in two fields of science – robotics and artificial intelligence. Robotics is the study of mechanical devices that function as some part of the human body or all of it. Artificial intelligence, called "AI" for short, goes inside the robot's computer. It is the software that provides the equivalent of brainpower. Scientists hope that with a mechanical body similar to a human's and a computerized brain similar to a human's, robots will be able to act, well … human – at least sort of.

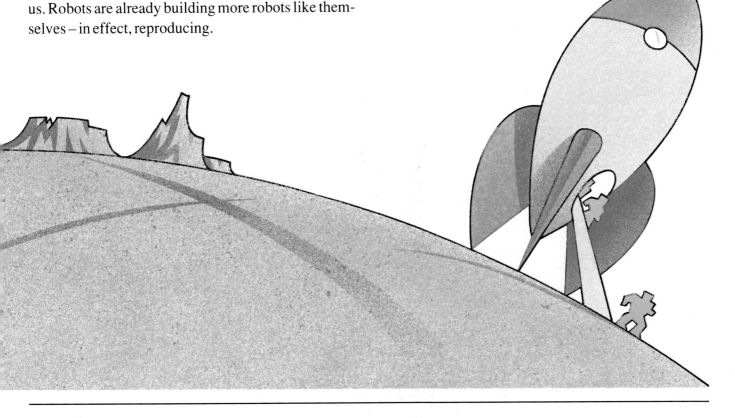

A computer by itself can't grip, see, pick up, or otherwise physically handle objects in the world. It essentially just sits on a desk, calculating at extremely high speeds and then feeding its answers to people. But with a human-like machine as its limbs and muscles, an intelligent computer of the future would be a radical development – a truly radical robot. It would be able to do many of the things we now think only people can do.

Making such a creation is one of the most difficult challenges facing scientists today. The metal or plastic body must be able to navigate safely through a world scattered with animals, small children, cars, rocks, bicycles, and toys, not to mention snow, wind, and rain. That is the robotics challenge.

And the computer controller inside must be able to tell the body what to do just as our brain instructs our arms and legs. But the human brain is a jungle of neurons interacting with each other in an astronomical number of ways. There is no means known to build a machine that complex. Scientists don't even know for sure how the brain's 100 billion neurons produce thinking, so it is extremely difficult to create a computer to function like this incredible organ. That is the artificial intelligence challenge.

A young man carefully controls a robotic arm in the delicate operation of picking up a pear.

Pick and Place

Why do we even need intelligent robots? Aren't there enough humans in this world to do all the work and make all of the decisions?

Scientists are creating robots to do jobs too dangerous, bothersome, or even too difficult for people to do themselves. In the summer of 1989, a robotic vehicle dove deeper into the Atlantic Ocean than any human could. Its task was to raise gold bars and rare coins from a paddle-wheel steamer that sank in a hurricane more than 100 years ago. A robot vehicle named Rover 1 entered the highly radioactive buildings of the Three Mile Island nuclear reactor after the accident there in 1979. And robot space machines are being designed to explore the universe, going where humans cannot yet go.

Most of the world's 200,000 robots are not so glamorous as these underwater divers and planetary voyagers. The ordinary robot is just a mechanical arm doing assembly-line work, such as "pick-and-place" operations that are very boring for human workers. Twenty-four hours a day these robotic arms can pick up a product – a can of soup, for instance – and place it in a box for shipment.

Sometimes these industrial robots come with extra thumbs and fingers, or even with suction cups, for better gripping. Others don't have fingers at all if designed to do just one thing, such as welding or spray-painting cars as they roll down an assembly line. In these cases, the jobs can be done by an arm with a tool fixed on the end. There's no need for a hand, either human or robotic, to hold the tool.

Human operators work in a safe, non-radioactive area of the Three Mile Island nuclear plant . . .

. . . while Rover cleans up in the dangerous contaminated area.

To the Drawing Board

The typical home robot differs greatly in concept from its industrial cousins. The most important distinction is that it is designed to do many different things, not just one job.

When perfected, such a multi-purpose robot may turn out to be a better helper around the house than you are. It will run on cheap battery power, handle many different chores without complaint, never need new clothes, never sleep, never forget, and never ask for an allowance. But there's one bad habit it has to break – running over the family cat.

Teaching a robot to avoid obstacles is not as easy as you might think. To understand the challenges scientists face in building a robot safe enough for your home and cat, let's go to the drawing board.

First, write down the things you would want a robot to do for you and your family.

Set the dinner table and wash the dishes? Unfortunately, it may be a century before your parents will trust a robot to touch their good china.

But how about carrying out the trash? That chore is pretty easy. With its mechanical arm, a robot can easily haul your trash bags down the driveway to the curb – as long as no skateboards lie in the way.

There are dozens of other household jobs, such as vacuuming the rugs, answering the phone and recording messages, and turning lights and heat on or off according to your programmed instructions. Your robot could guard your house against a fire or break-in and automatically dial the firehouse or police station should it detect trouble.

You might like your robot to go to school with you, carrying your books, reminding you of homework assignments, or recalling facts on the Civil War for you from its encyclopedic memory.

On the weekend, you might sometimes need a friend to play checkers or chess with you. Of course, your robot would have no trouble beating you 100 times out of 100, so the games wouldn't be much fun unless you set it at the "beginner's" level. You could play Nintendo on its video screen or learn about flight by watching videos on space missions.

Now that you have some sense of what a robot could do for you, draw on a piece of paper how you think one should look.

The Three Laws of Robotics

In his 1942 science fiction story "Runaround," writer Isaac Asimov proposed three rules for governing the actions of all robots:

1 A robot may not injure a human being or, through inaction, allow a human being to come to harm.

2 A robot must obey the orders given it by human beings except where such orders would conflict with the First Law.

3 A robot must protect its own existence as long as such protection does not conflict with the First or Second Law.

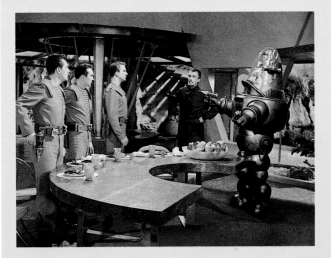

Robbie the Robot confronts earthlings in the movie "Forbidden Planet."

Arok – 275 pounds (124 kg.) of auto parts and household appliances – became a butler, waiter, dog walker, and carpet vacuumer in the hands of inventor Ben Skora in Palos Hills, Illinois.

A robot waiter brings food to the table in a Tokyo restaurant.

Just Like You

More than likely you have drawn a shiny metallic-looking creature with a head, body, two arms, two hands, and two legs. You probably decided to hide the computer brain inside its chest area behind a video screen and use TV cameras for eyes. Perhaps you put sound detectors on the sides of the head and covered the whole body in a touch-sensitive skin.

Look at what you have drawn – a robot that looks strikingly like you!

More precisely, you have probably drawn a picture of one of the only robots you know – C3P0 from the *Star Wars* movie. This celluloid marvel actually doesn't look too amazing when you open it up – there's a real live actor inside. No real robot today can match the movements, intelligence, and speaking ability of this beeping sheet of metal.

Now let's wipe the *Star Wars* stars from our minds and try again: what would the ideal robot look like?

How about a head that swivels 360 degrees, or eyes on the front and back? Why not three arms for those occasions when two can't carry enough? And the fingers – it might be handy to have them bend backward as well as frontward for gripping hollow objects from the inside.

C3P0 and pal R2D2 wander the woods in "Return of the Jedi."

A movie poster shows how humans reacted when nine-foot-tall Gort visited Earth in "The Day the Earth Stood Still."

Hollywood Robots

"Look, Dave," says HAL the computer to the human astronaut in the movie *2001*, "I can see you're really upset about this. I honestly think you ought to sit down calmly, take a stress pill, and think things over. I know I've made some very poor decisions recently."

In Hollywood's version of robots and computers, intelligence is taken for granted. In the above speech, HAL senses that Dave is angry. HAL seems to have a certain self-aware-ness, too, when he admits that he has made poor decisions. The idea that HAL has the mind and the freedom to make good or bad decisions is another film fantasy.

Just as human heroes are often exaggerated in movies and books, so are robots. Sometimes they are pictured humorously, like the androids in Woody Allen's movie *Sleeper*.

Robot gunslingers at an amusement park attack the human visitors in *Westworld*. In Fritz Lang's 1926 German film, *Metropolis*, a mad scien-tist schemes to replace human workers with smart machines.

Gort, a nine-foot robot from outer space, threatens to de-stroy the planet if humans don't stop testing the atomic bomb in *The Day the Earth Stood Still* (1951).

In *Forbidden Planet* (1956), Robbie the Robot (who knows 188 languages and cooks and sews) refuses to turn his ray gun on a human, thus obeying Isaac Asimov's first law. (See page 9, "The Three Laws of Robotics").

Isn't it odd that in so many films, the origins of the robots are rarely revealed? And why, if robots such as R2D2 and C3P0 are such wonderful creations, didn't the humans in these movies build more of them?

A more realistic view of robot capabilities comes from Asimov in his short story called "Little Lost Robot," published in 1947. A human casually tells a robot to "get lost," and this literal-minded machine obedi-ently goes off to do just that—get lost.

Renegade computer Hal reads astronauts' lips through a window as they plot against him in a sound-proof room, in the movie "2001: A Space Odyssey."

Woody Allen impersonates one of the androids – automa-tons resembling humans – which appear in his movie "Sleeper."

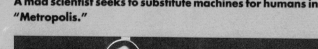

The face looks real, but underneath is an electronic gun-slinger in "Westworld."

A mad scientist seeks to substitute machines for humans in "Metropolis."

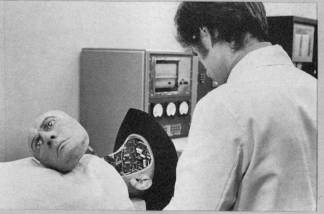

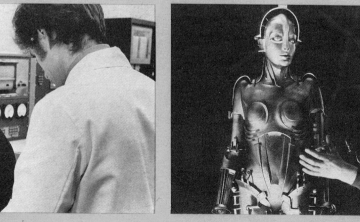

Instead of giving the robot just "perfect" eyesight, you could install X-ray vision for seeing inside objects and infrared vision for sensing objects in the dark. An ultrasonic transmitter would allow the robot to use echoes to determine precisely how far away an object is, distances that we can only approximate.

When it comes to legs, how about six for better stability, as some insects have? After all, two legs are really not very efficient for moving around. Just watch a small child learning to walk and you will see the quick adjustments the body must make at every step to keep from falling. You walk in the same way – you're just so much better at it that you aren't aware of the constant messages your brain sends to your muscles to keep you balanced.

Instead of legs, perhaps you would choose rubber treads like those on a tractor or tank. They would give your robot the best stability and traction. But treads would tear up the living room rug. Wheels create the smoothest movement, but they can't step over objects the way legs can.

So which would you put on your robot – two legs, six legs, treads, wheels, or something else?

Clayton borrows its form and mode of movement from an army tank.

Four bending legs allow this walking vehicle to negotiate rough terrain.

Robocycle's wheels carry the electronic brains of the vehicle.

Easy for You

The human body, brain, and senses evolved together over millions of years. But since scientists are starting from scratch designing robots, it doesn't make sense for them to build human weaknesses into what could be a superhuman machine.

So the ideal robot might not end up looking human-like at all. But it will need to act human in many ways. For instance, you would expect your robot to understand anyone talking to it, even if the person spoke with a southern drawl or a foreign accent. You would also assume that it could tell a dog from a cat and you from your friends. That sounds simple, but no machine can do it today.

In fact, one of the curious facts about robots is how easy it is for them to do what we find hard, and how hard it is for them to do what we find easy. The day a robot has the vision and coordination to tie shoelaces – something you learned before kindergarten – will be one of the greatest moments of science. Another great moment will come when a twelve-year-old flies aboard a spaceship to Mars just as a robot can today.

Scientist Marvin Minsky from the Massachusetts Institute of Technology (MIT) in Cambridge, Massachusetts, says that our brains devote billions of neurons to recognizing objects, which makes the task easy for us. Only a tiny fraction of our neurons is geared to solving mathematical problems, which makes that task hard for us.

Thousands of connections – compared with the billions in the human brain – form an integrated circuit board, which powers computers.

Billions of cells make up the human brain; information in the form of nerve impulses is transmitted and received by means of chemicals which bridge extremely small gaps, called synapses, between cells.

What You Can Do that a Robot Can't – and Vice Versa

You can ride a bicycle. A robot can't.

A robot can tell you the day of the week for any date you pick, such as your birthday. You must check a calendar.

You can climb a mountain and swim in a lake. A robot can't.

A robot can instantly add 142,792 and 43,341, multiply by 7, and say whether the resulting number is divisible by 3. You can't.

You can hear the sound of a dime dropping and crawl under the bed to retrieve it. A robot can't.

A robot can see in the dark. You can't.

You can recognize yourself in the mirror. A robot can't.

A robot can operate elevator doors by aiming an infrared beam. You can't.

You can feel a fly land on your cheek. A robot can't.

A robot can store in its memory the name and number of everyone in the phone book. You can't.

You can dance. A robot can't.

Some calculations that are simple for a computer can't even be done by the brain – unless you are a genius. Writer Isaac Asimov asks you to try dividing 72,647 by 323 – in your head! "You might walk from New York to Chicago in less time than it would take you to get the right answer," he says. A computer would do it faster than you can blink.

A computer is best at solving the problems that require rapid calculations and a vast memory – exactly what the human brain finds most troublesome. The human body easily accomplishes actions that use the brain, the eyes, and the hands because they have evolved to work together. Robots have great difficulty coordinating machine eyes with machine hands even if they are directed by a sophisticated computer.

So while you may never divide large numbers in your head, a robot might never learn to tie shoelaces. Still, each of you acts intelligently in different ways. You and the robot are at your worst doing what the other finds easy, and at your best doing what the other finds hard.

In other words, robots and humans seem to need each other.

A Cray 2, one of the world's most powerful supercomputers.

encyclopedia, compendium of knowledge, either general (attempting to cover all fields) or special (aiming to be comprehensive in a particular field). Basically it differs from a dictionary in that a dictionary is fundamentally devoted to words, an encyclopedia to information on subjects, with some data and some discussion of each subject identified. In actual practice this distinction is not kept clear; many dictionaries include some encyclopedia information, many (especially European) encyclopedias include entries that are no more than definitions. The terms are used confusingly in the titles of many modern reference books, and many special encyclopedias may be called dictionaries, manuals, handbooks, guides, companions, or the like. Distinction between encyclopedia and almanac is somewhat clearer, for an almanac normally is issued periodically and always includes ephemeral data applicable only at the time of issue, while an encyclopedia is always assembled within a broader scope. Attempts at encompassing universal knowledge began with the brilliantly comprehensive works of Aristotle. Other writers of the ancient world tried to follow his example, and sometimes the *Natural History* of Pliny the Elder is called the first encyclopedia. Alexandrian scholars in compiling their lengthy anthologies and summations of knowledge did some work of encyclopedic nature. The Oriental encyclopedias, particularly the voluminous Chinese collections, were actually more in the nature of anthologies than of reference works. In the Middle Ages various scholars drew up compendiums of knowledge; notable were the *Etymologae* of Isidore of Seville, a curious mixture of fact, half fact, and legend, and three 13th-century works by Vincent of Beauvais, Roger Bacon, and Brunetto Latini. William Caxton in 1481 printed an English translation of the encyclopedia of Vincent of Beauvais as *Mirror of the World*, and Caxton's successor, Wynkyn de Worde, printed an English translation to Joh... cyclopedia of natural science written in Latin (c.1250) by Bartholomew de Glanville. The modern type of encyclopedia – with alphabetical arrangement and frequently with bibliographi... ...acteristic form is usually said to have been first clearly established by John Harris in his *Lexicon technicum*, published in 1704. Ephraim Chambers in 1728 published his notable *Cy*... ...tion. In German, Johann Zedler published (1732-50) a *Universal-Lexikon*. Then came the most renowned of all encyclopedias, the French Encyclopédie (see separate article), wh... ...derot and others. The first edition of the *Encyclopedia Britannica* appeared in three volumes at Edinburgh in 1771. It grew in size and reputation over the years; despite its name... ...States. The oldest German encyclopedia still being published is *Brockhaus' Konversations-Lexikon*, first issued in 1796-1808. On this, rather than on the work of Ephraim C... ...ambers's Encyclopedia* (1st ed., 1859-68). The first noteworthy American encyclopedia was *The Encyclopaedia Americana*, edited by Francis Lieber (13 vols., 1829-33). A... ...nt. became more and more specialized, encyclopedias tended to be more numerous and more massive; they also gained more in value as tools because the terms used in a pa... ...unintelligible to scholars outside that field. Several new German and French encyclopedias appeared, as did the *Enciclopedia Italiana* (36 vols., 1929-39). Notable was the larg... ...*ya Entisiklopediya* [great Soviet encyclopedia] (1st ed., 65 vols.,

MF

Memorizing the Encyclopedia Doesn't Make You Intelligent

The word "robot" was first used in a play called *R.U.R.*, written seventy years ago by a Czechoslovakian named Karel Capek. The playwright derived "robot" from the Czech word for "forced labor" because his fictional machines were invented by people to do their dirty work.

In the play, the Rossum's Universal Robots company mixes vats of special substances to build the liver, brain, and other organs. A spinning wheel weaves the nerves and veins. The resulting robots look like humans and work like superhumans until the creation formula is tampered with. Emotions are added to the mix, and then the robots decide that they should not be slaves to their inferior creators. The robots rebel and kill off the human race.

At one point, *R.U.R.*'s general manager, Domin, says about the machine-like creatures, "They have astonishing memories, you know. If you were to read a twenty-volume encyclopedia to them, they'd repeat it all to you with absolute accuracy. But they never think of anything new."

有，"定之方中，作于楚宫"的记述冬前后初昏时分见于正南天空，这结果，开始进入冬闲了。所以，这定星出现在正南天空时，人们可《诗·幽风》："七月流火，九月授参中"。四月"初昏南门正"，五月

Проходим над Гималаями. Видим хребты с высочайшими вершинами мира. На краю долины Катманду, вытянувшейся с севера на юг, нашел Эверест. Как много людей мечтает

في اليوم الأول من مدارنا حول الأرض كان كل منا يشير إلى بلده عند مرورنا فوقها... ولكن مع مرور الأيام وعلى وجه التحديد في اليوم الثالث أو الرابع بدأ كل منا يشير إلى قارته... ومع قدوم اليوم الخامس لم نلاحظ حتى القارات وبدأنا نظر إلى الأرض كوكب واحد.

Capek was looking into the future, as science fiction writers often do. In 1921, electronic computers did not exist. Today the fastest supercomputers can do several billion calculations per second and easily store the contents of an encyclopedia, just as the fictional robots could do seventy years ago. The problem is, as Capek's character said, the robots still "never think of anything new."

A robot that can think of something new and react intelligently to new situations is the great goal of research. Right now robots work mostly where their environment can be tightly controlled, such as inside a warehouse or factory. These places are often rearranged to help the robot maneuver.

No such accommodation can take place in the outside world. Walking to the street corner is as dangerous for a mobile robot as walking through a mine field is for a soldier. Unforeseen occurrences – which humans adjust to every minute of the day – can easily trip up robots.

This robot can hold a newspaper, but it can't really read the articles.

In the stage production of "R.U.R.," actors play the roles of the rebellious slave robots.

When Sparrows Can't Fly

What we know today as computers were called "electronic brains" when invented forty five years ago. At that time, "computer" referred to a person who added numbers, such as a bookkeeper. Soon people realized that the new machine really wasn't figuring out problems the way a brain does. It was just computing numbers the way a bookkeeper did. So "computer" was a better name than "electronic brain." Today everyone uses the word "computer" to refer to a machine that computes rather than a person who computes.

One of the first computers was called "ENIAC," finally completed in 1946. This huge machine weighed 30 tons (27,210 kg), was 10 feet (3.048 m) high and 100 feet (30.48 m) long, and used 17,000 vacuum tubes to do its figuring. It was originally designed to enable soldiers in the field in World War II to calculate the path of projectiles. The machine did in thirty seconds what a skilled human computer took twenty hours to do.

Today you can buy a home computer more powerful than ENIAC. And you can program into it many facts of life. For instance: Most birds fly. A sparrow is a bird. The computer could put these two bits of information together and respond, if asked by a human, that a sparrow probably can fly, even though no one actually programmed in that fact.

Today personal computers more powerful than ENIAC can be run by schoolchildren.

ENIAC – called an "electronic brain" when it was invented in the mid-1940s – filled up many rooms and could only be operated by specialists.

A Timeline of Robotics and Artificial Intelligence

1921
Karel Capek's play, *R.U.R.* (for Rossum's Universal Robots) is produced in Prague, Czechoslovakia, the first recorded use of the word "robot."

1939
At the New York World's Fair, Westinghouse exhibits Elektro, a giant robot accompanied by his robot dog, Sparko. ▼

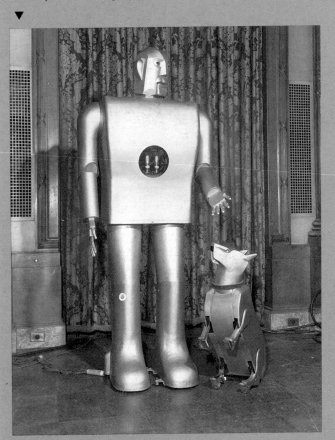

1939
The January edition of *Amazing Stories* publishes writer Eando Binder's "amazing confession," called "I, Robot" – perhaps the first story written from a robot's viewpoint. ▲

1942
Isaac Asimov publishes his three laws of robotics in the story "Runaround."

1954
George Devol builds the first industrial robot, a huge mechanical version of a human's arm, and later earns a patent for his invention.

1956
The field of artificial intelligence is born at a conference convened by John McCarthy at Dartmouth College in New Hampshire. ▼

1958
Joseph Engelberger (below) and George Devol found the world's first robotics firm, Unimation, Inc., a contraction of "universal" and "automation." ▼

1961
Unimation installs the first working industrial robot, Unimate 001, in a General Motors plant.

1966
Scientist Joseph Weizenbaum devises Eliza, a computer program that mimics the way a psychiatrist talks to patients. Eliza performs so well that people talk to her as if "she" were real.

1968
The first mutinous computer, HAL, appears in the science fiction movie, *2001: A Space Odyssey*.

1969
Stanford Research Institute in California builds SHAKEY, a wobbly moving robot that integrates wheels, sensors on its bumpers, a swiveling head, a TV camera eye, and a radio link to a computer. More importantly, SHAKEY could reason its way toward a goal, planning a route and moving obstacles out of its way if necessary. ▲

1976
Viking 1 lands on Mars, and its robotic arm takes soil and atmospheric samples. Because of the great distance to the red planet, it can take thirty minutes or more for the control signal from earth to reach the robotic arm. ▲

1977
The *Star Wars* movie introduces R2D2 and C3P0 to the world.

1981
"Factory Robot Kills Worker" reads the headline describing the first reported death caused by a robot. A robot cart runs over thirty-seven-year-old Kenji Urada in a Japanese factory while he is trying to repair the machine.

1982
Time magazine names the computer its annual "Man of the Year."

1982
RB Robot Corp.'s RB5X (below) becomes the first commercially available personal robot. Health Company also comes out with Hero 1. ▼

1983
Odetics, Inc. unveils its six-legged Odex-1, the first commercially available walking robot. ▼

1986
The robotic vehicle Jason, Jr. explores the wreckage of the ocean-liner Titanic under the Atlantic. ▼

1988
Roscoe, a robot, joins the staff of Danbury Hospital in Connecticut as a nurse's helper.

1989
The Soviet Union's Gary Kasparov, the world's best human chess player, defeats Deep Thought, the world's best computer chess program.

Fly a Kite

It's Saturday morning, a beautiful windy fall day outside. You don't have anything to do. Suddenly the phone rings and your friend Barbara says, "Do you want to go fly my kite with me?"

Perhaps you have flown a kite before, but maybe not. Either way, images flood through your brain. What do you think about? Wind first, of course, and an open field for running with the kite. Write down what comes to mind, then ask your mother to do the same.

Did you mention string, paper, and wood – what kites are usually made of? Did you think of how kites can crash if the wind is too gusty, or of the best places to fly, such as at the beach? What did your mother write down that you didn't mention?

If you ask two or three other people, won't you have to keep adding to the list of facts about kites?

Now think of yourself as a robot designer and decide what facts or rules about kites you would put into its computer memory.

Think of all you know about flying a kite, even if you have never actually done it.

What the computer lacks is a true understanding of what a sparrow is – why it can fly and when it can't. And the computer doesn't have your common sense. You know, of course, that sparrows with broken wings can't fly; sparrows caught in the mouth of a cat can't fly; dead sparrows can't fly, nor can newborn sparrows, or birds that are trapped in a box or held in your hands. The possibilities are so numerous and varied that it would be virtually impossible to feed into the computer all the exceptions to the fact that sparrows fly.

Think about how a friend might answer when you ask what he did on Saturday night. If he says, "I went to a restaurant," you know without thinking that he and his parents probably drove to a building, sat down, scanned the menu, ordered a meal, ate it, paid the bill, and left a tip. All of that information is implied in the five words "I went to a restaurant." You know so much about restaurants because you have gone to them yourself. You learned by induction – experience.

Induction taught you the principle of gravity even before you learned in school that it refers to the force that attracts objects to the center of the earth. You saw how a baseball drops to the ground if it isn't caught, or how leaves fall from a tree, or a book slides off a desk to the floor. From these experiences you understood that all things fall toward the earth unless something supports them. (Of course, balloons and airplanes are exceptions – a fact that you also learned by observation.)

Never programmed to know about gravity, a computer at MIT tried to build a pyramid out of children's blocks – from the top down.

Scientist Marvin Minsky, of MIT, learned a lesson about induction and robots during the late 1960s when he attached a computer to a mechanical arm and TV camera. He programmed the machine to analyze a stack of children's blocks and then rebuild it after he had knocked the stack down. Minsky's device seemed to recognize the pattern of the blocks correctly – the shapes, corners, edges, and so on. However, the mechanical arm tried to build the stack from the top down. It kept dropping the blocks into midair. But what could be expected from a machine that had never been programmed to know the principle of gravity?

F

Much of a Poet

...n't learn through experience as we do. Every-... knows about the world must be taught to it by h...ans. Since there are far too many facts to be programmed in, AI researchers specify general rules and hope the computer will deduce – figure out – the facts as well as the exceptions.

Unfortunately, many things can't be broken down into simple rules. Can you describe what it feels like to swim? Or how you recognize your mother in a crowd of faces sitting in the stands at a football game? Or how you know whether a loud sound outside is a car backfiring, thunder, or something else?

Isaac Asimov says, "That is the glory of the human brain – it can do things for which we are not yet able to write the rules."

Even where the rules are straightforward, the robot still can't match the human. Every rule of grammar and the meaning of every English word can be programmed into a computer. But then, can we expect the robot to be creative enough to write a poem?

Two professors at Allegheny College in Pennsylvania, Alfred Kern and Jim Sheridan, developed a program to get a computer to create poetry. Here is the machine's attempt:

You do remain autumn before any session
Unless shock gain coldly lemon autumn
You can silence during half silence
Despite silence freeze loosely accountable moment
For who would write than last sun
Herself count countless body
But who holds then mad tomb
Or who arrange unsure light
Provided marble teach adrift finite force

The computer put words together all right, but they don't make much sense.

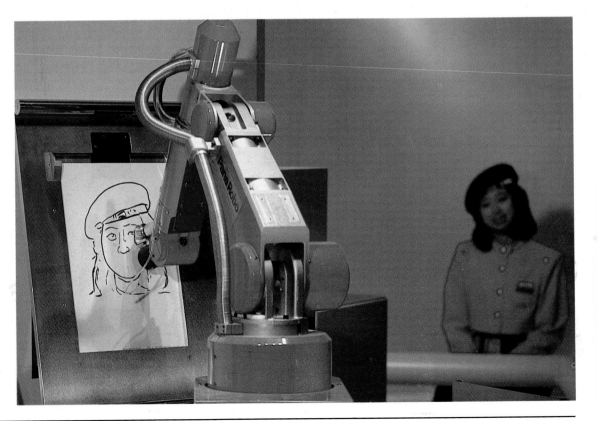

This robotic arm has been programmed to draw.

Your Move

Tic-tac-toe is a simple game that every child knows how to play. The first player picks one of nine spots to place his X or O. The next player has eight remaining choices. After he plays, there are seven moves left, then six, and so on.

You can figure out that there are 362,880 different moves that could be made – just multiply 9x8x7x6x5x4x 3x2x1. A computer can play tic-tac-toe like a champion because it can consider all the options in less than a second.

But let's increase the standard 3-square by 3-square board to 4 by 4. Suddenly the number of possible moves jumps to 20,000,000,000, 000 (20 trillion). If the board goes to 5 by 5, there are 15 million million million million possibilities. The computer could start calculating now and keep going until the universe ends. There still wouldn't be enough time to consider all the options.

Checkers is even more complicated. A fast computer could analyze one million options a second and still take 300,000,000,000,000,000, 000,000,000 years to consider all possible moves. In chess, there are estimated to be more possible moves than there are atoms in the universe!

Five-square tic-tac-toe, checkers, and chess illustrate a phenomenon of numbers called the "combinatorial explosion." Whenever in a game or problem one choice leads to two or more other choices, which lead to two or more other choices, and so on, the options build up so quickly that no computer can try out every possibility.

So not even the fastest supercomputers can make decisions by using this "brute force" method of considering every possibility. For checkers or chess, the machine must rely on rules, just as humans do, to eliminate the unlikely options.

In everyday life, the choices open to you can "explode" just as fast as in a game. For instance, when you wake up on a Saturday morning, you might go to the bathroom, brush your teeth, take a shower, get dressed, go downstairs, find cereal, pour milk, eat, and go outside to ride your bike. Or maybe you go to the bathroom, brush your teeth, get dressed, eat a muffin for breakfast, and decide to do your Saturday chores first. Or you could get dressed first, then brush your teeth, go downstairs, eat eggs for breakfast, and call up a friend to go play soccer.

There are few rules for getting up on Saturday morning or doing many other ordinary activities. That's what makes it so hard to tell a computerized robot how we live – or how it can maneuver through such a complicated human world.

Rules of Thumb

Scientist Douglas Lenat at the Microelectronics & Computer Technology Corp. in Austin, Texas, is working on the common-sense side of the machine-intelligence problem. In a project called "Cyc" – short for encyclopedia – he is trying to instill in a computer what every child entering school knows.

At the end of this ten-year effort in 1994, Lenat expects to have programmed in 100 million assertions. Only one-third of this input will be facts. The rest will be the rules of thumb that an encyclopedia assumes you already know.

For instance, says Lenat, "Suppose that you saw your friend Fred riding his bicycle home from school. Later, your mother asks you how Fred got to school that day. You would probably say he rode his bike, because you know that people usually get home from a place the same way they went there."

You know this rule of thumb even though no one ever taught it to you. But Lenat's computer would never have known this rule if it hadn't been told.

If your alarm clock, telephone, refrigerator and other household appliances "knew" your schedule and could "talk" to each other, they could let you sleep late and have your breakfast ready at just the right time.

Lenat sees many possible applications for a computer program that understands how life works. For instance, imagine an alarm clock that knows you stayed up late the night before and don't want to be awakened until 9:00 A.M. If your phone rings at 8:00 A.M., Lenat says, "The alarm clock might discuss with the telephone whether you should be woken up or not." The alarm may decide to let you sleep until 9:00 A.M. When it rings then, you might try to turn it off to get more sleep. But the alarm knows your schedule – you have a piano lesson at 10:00 A.M. – and so keeps ringing anyway.

A common-sense refrigerator, Lenat speculates, could print out messages on the front door: "The strawberries are five days old" or "Check if you have enough milk." A refrigerator programmed to know your calendar might realize on a Thursday that it needed to start making extra ice for a big party you have scheduled for Saturday.

Writers Donald Michie and Rory Johnston give a good example in *The Knowledge Machine* of something simple an intelligent robot should be capable of doing if it had the common sense of a five-year-old. Let's say the robot is told two things: "Clyde is an elephant," and "Clyde is sitting in the back row of the movie theater." A useful computer, like a child, should immediately respond, "That's crazy!"

Here's Two You

Besides understanding the world through experience, humans also take in knowledge by reading, listening, and even touching. Robots can't do any of these well yet. Writer George Gilder says in his book, *Microcosm*, "It takes the most advanced computer hours or even days to accomplish feats of seeing and hearing that are routinely performed (instantly) by human eyes and ears."

The major limitation is power. Professor Jacob Schwartz of New York University in Manhattan estimates that even the most advanced current computers "are probably no more than one four-millionth as powerful as the human brain . . . and have no more than about one four-millionth of the memory capacity" as well.

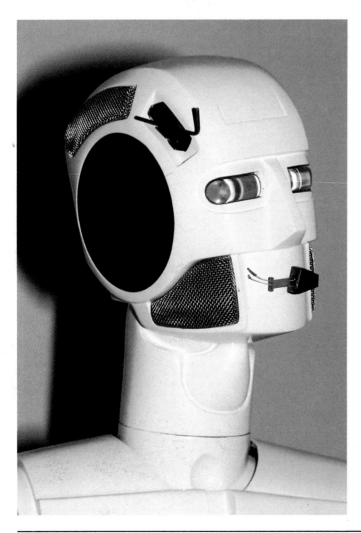

Our senses help each other, too. Seeing a person's mouth and gestures and expressions helps us to understand his or her words. Our sense of smell adds to our sense of taste. So it isn't just a matter of developing good individual senses in a robot; these senses would have to work together if the robots are to match humans.

When it comes to gripping, for example, your hand automatically adjusts the pressure to the object. You wouldn't squeeze an egg in the same way you would a baseball. But a robot today doesn't know the difference between the two. It must use special feedback systems so that its fingers apply just the right amount of force so as not to crush the egg or drop the baseball.

Understanding human speech requires a lot of processing power by a computer. For instance, the words "to," "two," and "too" sound alike although they mean different things. Computers can be programmed to figure out which one a person is using by the other words in the sentence. When you say "I went to the ballgame" you don't mean "I went *two* the ballgame." An advanced speech recognition system today can understand that you mean "Please give me two cartons of milk" rather than "*too* cartons," but it can't yet understand your meaning quite as fast as you can speak the words.

If it is to function "intelligently," a robot needs ways to take in information about the world as humans do – through our eyes, nose, ears, mouth, and skin.

Tricky Words

There are more tricky problems of language. If the robot hears the word "six" in the sentence "There are six . . .," it naturally expects the next word to be some object of which there are six. But if the robot then hears the sound "teen," it will put the "six" and "teen" together and expect that there are sixteen of something. Now consider what happens if the following sound is "agers." The computer must backtrack again to understand that "there are six teenagers working in the record store."

People often slur their words together, use slang or pet words instead of the real names for things, and say what they don't mean. If you told your father, "I could run a marathon in two hours," he might say, "You're all wet," meaning that you are foolish to think that. A robot listening in would figure that you are soaked. The many complications of language make it hard for even powerful computers to understand human speech.

The rules that researchers program into computers are logical. But think of the odd connections that the human brain makes. If I say "play" to you, what do you think of – a game, a toy, a musical instrument, or maybe even a play on stage at school? Now think of that one game or toy or instrument or stage play – what do you think of next? That you won the game, lost the toy, hit the wrong note, or starred in the stage play? Your mind may connect from one thought to a dozen more in a few seconds.

Or maybe when I said "play" you said "raisins" for absolutely no reason you can think of. Did your mind make a mistake? Or were you eating raisins the last time you played checkers? The point is that how your mind works is governed by the structure of the brain as well as by your own individual experiences and memories contained in it.

Nobody knows exactly how we think as we do, and that makes it impossible right now to build a robot exactly like us.

If Computers Are So Smart, How Come They Didn't Invent Artificial Intelligence?

"Sometime in the next thirty years," says biologist James McAlear, "very quietly one day we will cease to be the brightest things on earth."

Robots have a long way to go to surpass human intelligence, but consider how fast the airplane developed. Grace Hopper, one of the first computer programmers, remembers riding in a biplane in 1924. "It was built out of linen, wire, and wood," she says. "I could no more have dreamt of a 747 than I could have jumped over the moon." Hopper certainly could not have dreamed that the biplane would evolve into a rocket so powerful it could take a human from Earth to the moon.

So the question is: What will today's infant robots grow into in your lifetime?

Think of the airplane again. Surely the inspiration to fly came to humans from watching birds soar through the air. Many people tried mimicking birds by strapping on wings and jumping off a mountain, flapping their arms as fast as they could. These daredevil inventors crashed hard.

The airplane that succeeded was not built as an exact model of a bird. Planes don't have flapping wings, and they don't take off and land on a dime. What inventors learned is that there is more than one way to fly. In fact, no bird can equal the power and speed of a supersonic jet. On the other hand, no plane can match the quick turns and dives of a bird.

The lesson of airplanes and birds applies to artificial intelligence and the brain. A robot does not need to be controlled by a computer that is modeled exactly like the human brain. Perhaps scientists can build a robot brain that works better in some ways than your brain, even though it might be worse in other ways.

Sometimes the word "artificial" indicates something not as good as the original, such as an artificial flower. But as Robert Sokoloski, professor of philosophy at Catholic University in Washington, D.C., notes, at other times something artificial can become valuable in its own right, such as artificial light. Researchers expect that artificial intelligence in robots will turn out like artificial light – special and important in its own way.

In the superficial shape of its body and wings, a jet looks somewhat like a bird, but otherwise has few similarities.

Movable, strong, light-weight wings allow a bird to fly by flapping or gliding.

A would-be aviator in the 1920s straps an unwieldy pair of wings on his back. (He didn't get off the ground.)

"My Robot is Better than Your Robot"

Scientists and engineers aren't the only ones building robots. Kids do, too.

Each spring the Society of Manufacturing Engineers sponsors a national Robotic Contest to encourage students to design, build, and program robots.

You don't need expensive materials, either, as long as you have imagination. One high school boy decided to build his entry out of the parts of a junked automobile – the sensors, electrical circuits, motor, and metal body. Others have used common Lego blocks or Tinker Toys for the body.

The Robotic Contest challenges middle- and high-school students in various ways. One task is to program a tabletop robot to pick up a stack of alphabet letters, bring them back, and form the word "ROBOT" out of them.

For the maze problem, contestants must build an automated robot "mouse" that can move along a path from beginning to end, including both left- and right-hand turns.

Another part of the contest asks students to build a robot to perform some specific task of their own choosing. Past entries have included robots that could mix chemicals or play tic-tac-toe. One winner developed an automated hamburger-making system. This industrial-type robot fried the meat, heated the bun, put the hamburger in the bun, added ketchup, then slid the finished burger down a tray for the counter person to deliver to the customer.

Contests can lead to a lifelong interest in a field. Scientist Hans Moravec of Carnegie-Mellon University was inspired by a science teacher in high school to enter a local science fair. He built Robug. "Its body was an upside-down salad bowl on wheels, propelled by old tape-recorder motors," Moravec writes in his book, *Mind Children*. He used three sensors to respond to light, and wrapped wire around the shaft of a screwdriver to create feelers. Robug won a blue ribbon in the school contest.

For information about this annual national robot competition, write to Robotic Contest, Society of Manufacturing Engineers, One SME Drive, Box 930, Dearborn, MI 48121.

An annual contest sponsored by the Society of Manufacturing Engineers invites kids of various ages to build robots.

The Vacuum Speaks

The first robots to come into the home in the 1990s will be semi-intelligent, according to Edward Cornish, president of the World Future Society. A robot vacuum might command, "Sofa Move. Chair Move." And those pieces of furniture would move themselves back a few feet so the vacuum can pass. A robot arm in the kitchen could be programmed to take food from the freezer and cook it in the microwave. A robot entertainer would sit in the den playing games with the family.

Sometime in the future, all of these job-specific robots will come under the control of a single general-purpose super-robot who orders them to their chores. This command machine will move about your house and yard freely, always monitoring, sensing, and calculating. Perhaps one day when your super-robot meets the neighbor's super-robot out at the curb, one might ask the other, "How many humans does it take to memorize the encyclopedia?"

A robot arm attached to your bathroom sink could brush your teeth for you and comb your hair, but these everyday activities are so easy that you wouldn't buy a robot to do them for you. Yet a handicapped person who has lost the use of an arm might well find these functions helpful.

On a cold, rainy day, you will be able to shop at the grocery story from your living room, says Cornish. The market will supply its own robots so you can tell them which products to retrieve. The robot might even hold bananas up to the camera for you to assess their ripeness, or even test the firmness of a melon and transmit the feeling through a robotic sleeve to your hand.

Test the Robot

Robotic arms will shear sheep and pump gas. Mobile robots will walk into a blazing house fire to rescue a family when the heat is too intense for a human firefighter.

In the early 1990s, Denning Mobile Robots, Inc. expects to sell machines that will guard parking lots, prisons, landing fields, and army storage facilities. The company has even been asked by ranchers if its Sentry robot could patrol the prairie to watch for cattle rustlers.

In the office, a robot mail clerk is technically possible already. But, says Warren George, Denning's chairman, people have unrealistic expectations – that the robot can be installed and do the job without any learning period. A human mail clerk is shown around the offices for a few days and allowed to make a few mistakes. Not so with the robot. People just turn it on and expect it to perform flawlessly. George says, "If a robot nicks a corner once in 500 times, people say it has failed. But look at how often a person bumps into a wall in the office. No one says the person is a failure."

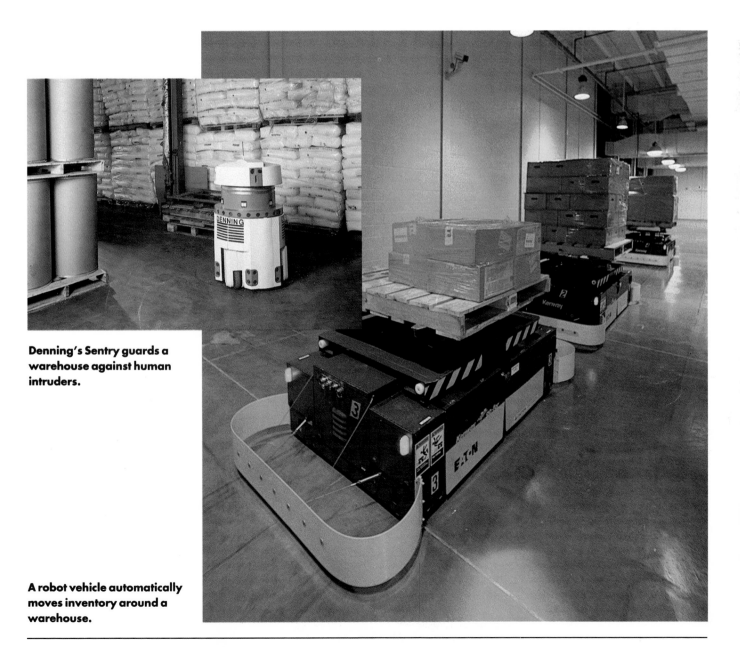

Denning's Sentry guards a warehouse against human intruders.

A robot vehicle automatically moves inventory around a warehouse.

Robots for Sale

A Hospital Orderly

If there is one place so chaotic that you would not expect to find a robot, it is a hospital. But that's exactly where Transitions Research Corp. is testing HelpMate.

At Danbury Hospital in Connecticut, Roscoe the transport robot maneuvers through the cluttered corridors, avoiding patients, doctors, wheelchairs, and beds. His job is to run errands. By punching in commands on a keypad, a nurse can send him to the stockroom to get more rubber gloves or to the kitchen to pick up a late meal tray for a patient.

Roscoe summons the staff elevator by an infrared beam (similar to the way you change TV channels by remote control) and finds his way through the hospital by means of a map in his memory.

You might lean against Roscoe in the corridor and not even realize that he is much more than a lifeless piece of equipment. The robot was designed to look boring – like an ordinary medical machine. The difference is that this one travels around the hospital on its own.

On Guard

Denning Mobile Robotics, Inc., in Wilmington, Massachusetts, sells a security robot named Sentry for about $50,000. Sentry patrols offices and warehouses, guarding against break-ins.

One of its sensing systems works by microwave. One day, Sentry discovered intruders breaking in through the roof of Boston's Bayside Exposition Center. The robot sent a warning signal to the human guard in his office, but the guard couldn't hear or see any trouble and so thought the robot was malfunctioning.

After a while, one of the intruders climbed from the skylight down to the warehouse floor and called to his accomplices, "It's okay, drop me the tools." What the criminal couldn't see in the dark was the 485-pound (219.705 kg) robot detecting him through its infrared beam. Sentry sent video pictures and radio signals back to the guard, who came out to chase the intruders.

If he preferred, the guard could have remained at his station and spoken through the robot's microphone. He might have said, "Please approach the robot and show your badge." Not many people would refuse an order coming from a strange-looking robot of unknown abilities.

Warren George, chairman of Denning, says Sentry will move around objects if its path is blocked, but never more than twenty or thirty feet (6.096 m or 9.144 m) from its programmed patrol. And can this robot go down stairs? "Yes," George jokes, "but only once."

Help for the Handicapped

Prab Command, Inc., of Kalamazoo, Michigan, makes a voice-controlled robotic arm that gives new abilities to the severely handicapped. Prab Voice Command I will obey such instructions as "Get book" or "Turn page." To a person without arms, this kind of help can make it possible to read and work, to use a computer, to make phone calls.

As a result of certain diseases, a person's speech can become slurred. Prab Command I doesn't mind. It can be trained to respond to any voice, as long as the words are said in the same way each time.

Prab Voice Command – an arm for people who cannot use their own.

HelpMate – a robot that fetches items for nurses in a hospital.

Robo-Surgeon

At the Long Beach, California, Memorial Medical Center, a robotic arm can do a kind of brain surgery. The PUMA 260 machine practiced on a watermelon. Then in 1985, it operated on its first human patient.

A computer instructs the robot arm where to position itself and drill. After the hole is made, the arm inserts a probe to take a tissue sample. The robot is so precise (to two one-thousandths of an inch) (.0508 mm) and quick that the patient spends much less time on the operating table.

The robotic hand may prolong the career of skilled surgeons whose own reflexes and control have slipped as they grow older. They can bring their experience to the operating room and let the robot handle some of the precision cutting.

Lawn Help

Technical Solutions, Inc., in Damascus, Maryland, demonstrates a robot that many a kid will love – an automated lawn mower. Lawn Ranger, as it is called, works on a simple premise – it moves toward higher grass. So all you need to do is cut the outside edge of your yard, and then Lawn Ranger will mow the rest in circles until it reaches the middle.

You might think trees would be a problem, but Technical Solutions came up with an ingenious solution. The homeowner just trims the grass around the trees, as he or she would do anyway. When Lawn Ranger comes along, it senses the shorter grass and turns away to cut the taller grass.

The machine is expected to cost between $1,000 and $1,500 when it comes to market in the next year or two. At that price, only businesses or people with lawns at least an acre (0.405 ha) in size would find Lawn Ranger worth the expense.

Droids and Dogs

Clap your hands, and Droid Genesis will come to you, if that's what you have programmed it to do. This voice- or sound-commanded household robot will sell for about $12,500. The one gripper hand can lift 12 pounds (5.436 kg).

The makers of this four-foot (1.2192 m) plastic robot believe that in the next few years it will be able to wash your car, answer the phone, tell jokes, serve food at parties, feed the pets, shovel snow, and water the plants.

For the sports-minded, the robot can carry your golf clubs like a caddy around the course or toss tennis balls over the net for you to practice your backhand.

The machine is meant to go outside as well – to walk the dog, for instance. Imagine seeing a little English terrier being walked down the street by a 150-pound (67.95 kg) Droid!

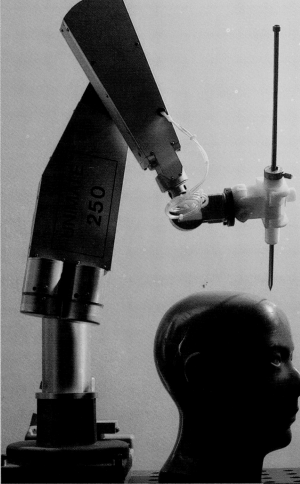

Robo-Surgeon – a mechanical arm that performs certain surgical cuts.

Lawn Ranger – help for the kid with a large lawn to cut.

People are always testing robots, too, giving them strange instructions. "People love to put masking tape over the sensors or throw things in front of a robot to see how it will react," says Gay Bogardus, director of marketing at Transitions Research Corp. (TRC). This potential vandalism worries robot makers who are trying to build foolproof machines.

Bogardus says that technically advanced dancing robots and stair-climbing robots are possible, but their price tag will make them unavailable for a long time. TRC's goal is Homebot, an automated vacuuming, cleaning, helper robot.

"In twenty years, no one is going to be mowing their own lawn," Bogardus believes, "or washing their own car, or cleaning their bathroom. This is not fantasy land. It's happening now."

Not Just for Engineers

Building robots used to be mostly a mechanical challenge requiring engineering skills. Computer scientists worked separately on the artificial intelligence problem.

But as these machines develop into semi-intelligent mobile robots traveling through uncontrolled situations and interacting with people, other fields come into play.

A manufacturer must consider how big to make the robot, what its speed and color will be, and whether it should look like an insect, a refrigerator, or an android. These so-called "human factors" help determine whether people accept robots working among them.

So robot-makers are looking for students graduating from college with degrees in psychology, sociology, and business, to help make basic design decisions.

Is it a robot or a dinosaur? Dinamation International Corp. in California merges the two into lifelike creatures.

Astrobots on Their Own

Robots – or astrobots – will carry human culture out into the universe where people cannot go yet. In the next century, spacecraft will head far beyond our solar system to distant planets. Even at the speed of light, radio transmissions could take days, weeks or even years to travel between earth and the spacecraft. A robot that is exploring the terrain can't wait for a year to get instructions from Earth as to whether it should keep going or stop. It might fall over a cliff by that time.

Carnegie-Mellon University in Pittsburgh, Pennsylvania, is building an eighteen-foot (5.4864 m)-tall rover to go to Mars for NASA in the 1990s. Instead of a body, the six-legged machine will have a round platform measuring six feet (1.8288 m) in diameter on which the radar, sonar, and other sensing devices can be mounted.

The university is also designing military robots for the U.S. Defense Department. For such an application, an autonomous robot would need to be able to follow a path, such as a road. But what is a road? Dr. Frank Pittman, associate director of Carnegie-Mellon's Robotics Institute, says, "You can tell the robot to look for two parallel edges and steer down the middle of them. The problem is that a tree trunk also has two parallel edges." The robot that runs into the nearest tree isn't going to be of much help on the battlefield.

So astrobots and military robots will need to take care of themselves and make decisions for themselves. In the past, if a computer did something it wasn't instructed to do, it was considered a mistake – a bug. But in the future we will want our computer-controlled robots to do things on their own, rather than just act like machines. In fact, if scientists are successful, "acting like a machine" may eventually come to mean "acting with intelligence."

At MIT's Artificial Intelligence Lab, researchers are developing microbots. These five-pound (2.265 kg) mechanical creepers will be cheap enough and small enough to fly on space missions. One of these, the eight-inch tall "Attila," as the six-legged creature is known, will be able to crawl up sixty-degree slopes, sense whether it is walking on sand or rock, and create its own map of the terrain so that it can choose the best path to travel. The front two legs will double as "hands" that can pick up objects and drop them over its back into a carry bag.

Around MIT's research labs, you never know what you will see. There's a pogo-stick robot that can do back flips, and the helpful Herbert, a robot designed to grab empty soda cans off desks and deposit them in the collection box for recycling.

A robot like this might go to Mars for NASA in the 1990s.

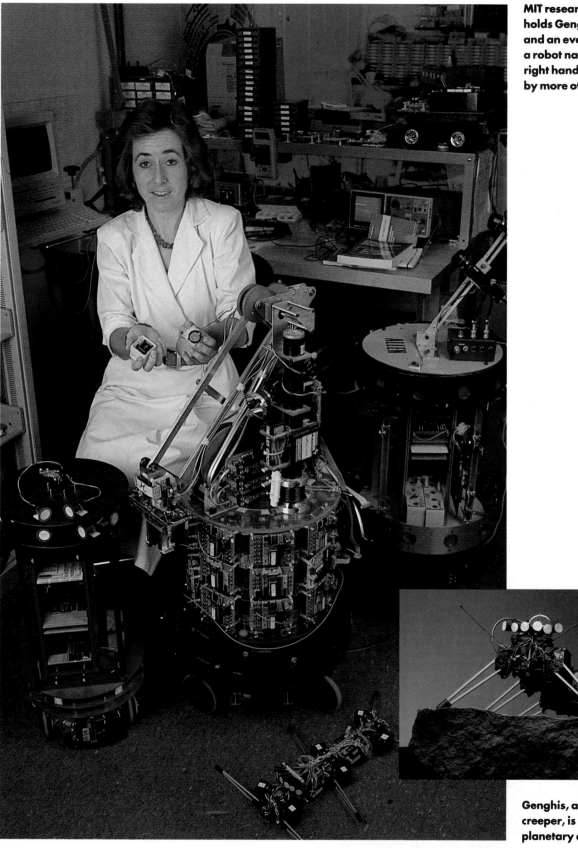

MIT researcher Anita Flynn holds Genghis in her left hand and an even smaller model of a robot named Squirt in her right hand. She is surrounded by more of her robot creations.

Genghis, a six-legged creeper, is MIT's idea for a planetary explorer.

You, Robot

Some researchers are pursuing a side trail on the way to creating the Radical Robot of the 21st century. In teleoperation, the robot acts not according to its own computer's instructions but on the orders sent by a person in another location. This person is wearing a robotic sleeve so that he or she can feel what the robot feels. The person also wears a helmet to hear what the robot hears and see what the robot's TV cameras see.

Because the person is sensing only what the robot does, he or she actually feels as if he or she is the robot moving around in that remote location. If the person sees an object that must be moved, he or she lifts his or her own hand to grab it – which signals the robot to do the same thing. In effect, the robot becomes a mechanical shell for a human to operate.

If teleoperation is perfected, you might rent a robot in Egypt, for instance, and signal it to go to the pyramids or the sphinx for you. You could learn your history lessons by experiencing these faraway places as if you were there.

If your family wanted to move to Phoenix, Arizona, you could use a robot to inspect houses for sale. Wearing the special helmet and sleeves, you could direct the robot through the house, seeing if you like the size of the kitchen or the location of your room.

Mattel Toys released a product in the fall of 1989 using the principle of teleoperation that NASA uses for controlling robots. The $80 Power Glove replaces the joystick on the popular Nintendo games. For instance,

in Mike Tyson's Punch-Out game, you can curl your fingers into a fist inside the Power Glove and aim at Tyson's face. The character on the screen will deliver the punch.

The signals that allow you to control a robot's arm could work in reverse as well. Suppose the robot's arm was programmed to swing a tennis racket the way Chris Evert does. The exact moves could be signaled to the sleeve you wear so that your arm would be guided in just the right way for you to learn Evert's swing.

Teleoperation is how humans control many robots today, such as the ones that go into nuclear plants or dive underwater. The researchers can spend less time trying to put intelligence into the robot and concentrate instead on building a better mechanical body. A human sitting a safe distance away provides the intelligence.

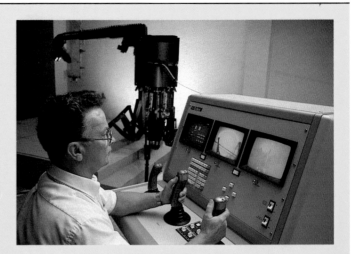

In the distant future, perhaps you could send your robot to school for you when you are sick.

Or imagine this strange situation: Two robots sit downstairs in your living room while you are upstairs. You put on the body suit that governs the arms and legs of one robot and put on the helmet that enables you to see what the second robot is looking at. Which would be the one with you in it?

At the Savannah River Nuclear Laboratory in South Carolina, an operator works the controls of a remote robot.

A man uses a special glove to manipulate objects on a computer screen.

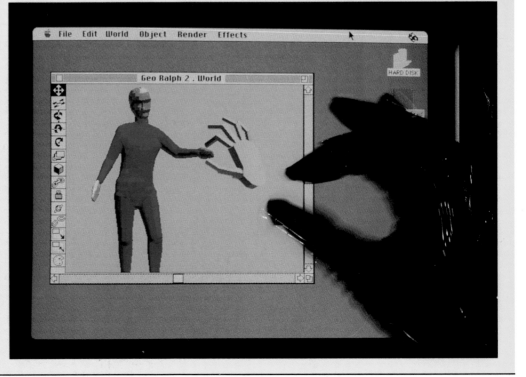

Robo-Criminals

As robots become smarter and more widely used, they create many tricky legal problems. A big runaway robot could in seconds create a door where there once was a wall.

What if your super robot told my lowly robot rug cleaner to vacuum my dog? Whose machine would be at fault?

Or what if you borrowed my robot lawn mower and it zigzagged out of control across your vegetable garden?

Human criminals sitting safely in a hideaway might use a robot to rob stores for them. Through tele-operation, the criminal could maneuver the machine down the sidewalk into the store, lift the robot's big hand, and threaten to crush the person behind the counter unless he turned over the money.

If a robot walking in town suddenly knocked a person down, the prosecuting lawyer would have to prove that the robot meant to do harm – which would be very hard to prove since robots don't really mean to do anything. The lawyer might try holding the robot's owner at fault, believing that the robot had been programmed to misbehave.

"Suppose," says Hans Moravec in his book *Mind Children*, a robot "finds itself locked out of its owners' home, its battery charge fading." The robot will search furiously for options to get a recharge. And it may barge through a screen door into a stranger's house looking for an electrical outlet.

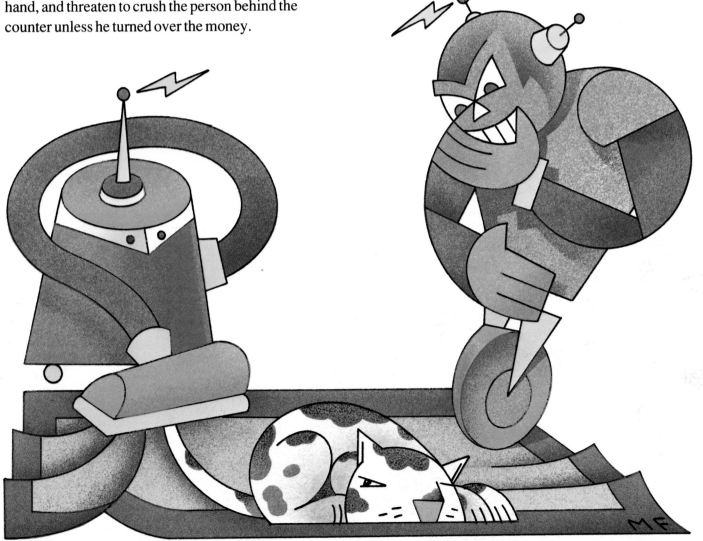

Moravec envisions an intelligent machine in the shape of a bush. Its rod-like body would branch off into arms, each of which would keep branching into a trillion smaller and smaller fingers. Such a machine would have the extraordinary ability to detect the slightest movements and the tiniest objects. It might be able to reach inside a machine, such as an airplane engine, or even inside a human body, and simultaneously sense and repair any part working incorrectly.

As his mind wanders to the far-out future, Moravec asks, "Is there any chance that we – you and I, personally – can fully share in the magical world to come?"

Yes, he answers, we could, by means of a mind transplant or brain scan. Today the ailing parts of a human can be replaced by an artificial arm or leg or even, sometimes, a heart. Perhaps the reverse could occur – the essence of the human brain could be transferred into the body of a robot.

The chemical composition and electrical impulses that make up your mind could be detected, he theorizes, and transferred to a computer program. The program would control a robot – the new you! It would think like you, remember like you, and act like you.

It might even live longer than you. But what then: Should the "robot you" be destroyed when you die?

From the mind of scientist Hans Moravec has come this bush-like robot of the future.

A Victory for Humans

Just as there are dog shows and horse competitions, there could be robot races and quizzes and puzzles to determine who owns the fastest and smartest robot in town.

In five years, a computer may be the best chess player in the world, according to the best human chess player today, Gary Kasparov. In October of 1989, this Soviet chess genius took on the best computer chess program, called Deep Thought. Kasparov felt that the reputation of human intelligence was at stake. He said, "I had to challenge Deep Thought to protect the human race."

Kasparov, who is considered the finest chess player who ever lived, won rather easily in 52 moves. But Deep Thought was only analyzing 720,000 positions a second. In five years, it will be 1,000 times faster!

Kasparov admits that he has a hard time accepting the idea that a computer chess program could someday be smarter than he is. As writer Arthur C. Clarke says, "There's an element of fear involved because this challenges and threatens us, threatens our supremacy in the one area in which we consider ourselves superior to all the other inhabitants of this planet."

Soviet chess star Gary Kasparov challenged a computer in 1989 – and won.

Machine intelligence may be a threat in another way. What if the super robots decide they are too smart to be our servants any longer? Might they revolt like Rossum's robots in Capek's science fiction play?

MIT's Joseph Weizenbaum points out that even when a robot learns to tell a cat from a dog, it still won't really know what a cat or dog is. All the robot will know about these animals is the list of attributes programmed into it. Humans not only know that a cat purring or a dog wagging its tail is friendly – they *feel* the friendliness. No machine will ever do that, says Weizenbaum.

If you are ever in doubt that people are smarter than computerized mobile robots, remember this: people are creating robots, robots aren't creating people. We can control them.

As Clarke says, "It is possible that we may become pets of the computers, leading pampered existences like lap dogs, but I hope that we will always retain the ability to pull the plug if we feel like it."

"Sometimes I ask myself, 'Where will it ever end?'"

Where to See Robots

If reading about robots makes you want to see or even build one, call up your local science and children's museums. Ask if they exhibit robots or sell "build-your-own" kits.

One particularly good exhibit is at The Computer Museum in Boston, Massachusetts, which demonstrates robots in its Smart Machines Theater. Twenty-five machines come to life as they are introduced in a ten-minute show. You can see Denning's Sentry, NASA's Mars Rover, and Stanford Research Institute's Shakey.

Elsewhere in the museum, you can type your name into a computer and watch a robotic arm spell it in blocks. Or, by the touch of a joystick, you can direct a foot-high robot on wheels around its pen.

The "Color the States" computer demonstrates speech recognition. The machine gives you the choice of four colors with which to paint a map of the United States, one color per state. You pick the state and announce your color, which the computer then fills in on its video screen. The challenge for the computer system is to understand all of the different accents among the museum's 100,000 yearly visitors. Your challenge is to complete the map without allowing

states of the same color to touch each other. (You can try this test – called the "Four-Color Problem" – at home with a map and four differently colored crayons.)

Another exhibit analyzes a two-minute conversation between Dave, the human, and HAL, the computer, in the movie, *2001*. This video reveals the incredible amount knowledge and intelligence HAL would have to possess order to speak as it does in film. The analysis concludes that scientists may build smart machines someday, but not by the year 2001.

Boston's Computer Museum has one of the largest collections of robots assembled anywhere.

Building robots isn't just for scientists. Kids of all sizes can create robots from kits or objects around the house.